CROSS PURPOSES

Meditations and Prayers based on meals with Jesus

by

Eddie Askew

By the same author:

A Silence and a Shouting
Disguises of Love
Many Voices One Voice
No Strange Land
Facing the Storm
Breaking the Rules

© The Leprosy Mission International
80 Windmill Road, Brentford
Middlesex TW8 0QH, UK

© Paintings and drawings A.D. (Eddie) Askew

A.D. (Eddie) Askew has asserted his right to be identified
as the author of this work

Published 1995

ISBN 0 902731 37 8

Printed by Stanley L. Hunt (Printers) Ltd, Rushden, Northants NN10 9UA

To Joyce and Dudley
with love.

Watercolour paintings and drawings by the author

Foreword

Thank you, Eddie, and keep them coming!

Breakfast in our home is never the same without a closing meditation and prayer from one of your lovely devotional books. It's a mistake to read more than one chapter at a time. Each needs to be savoured, with lingering appreciation, making each prayer one's own, even while we savour our last sips of coffee. When we finish the last chapter of each book, we sometimes go back and read them over again at more breakfasts, or go back to an earlier book: they just don't grow old.

Since you sent me the proofs of this new book in the series, I had to break my rules and peek ahead. I'm glad you have given more space to the meditations. It has brought new life and details to the stories. They come alive.

As for the prayers, I suppose that I had been afraid that after six books these might have started to become a little repetitive. I should have remembered the length and breadth and depth of your life and experience. I have known you as a missionary in India, working as a servant among leprosy patients; as a leader and director back in England, keeping a sense of humour in tough situations; as a family man; and as an artist, who sees beauty and displays it, where others have seen nothing special.

It all comes out in the down-to-earth insights and the poetry of the prayers. Who else could write:

> *I find it hard to look beyond the obvious,*
> *my mind so sealed*
> *it almost breaks imagination's fingernails*
> *to prise it open*
> *to the wonder of your presence.*

Thank you, Eddie, and keep them coming!

Paul Brand

Dr Paul Brand CBE MB FRCS is known throughout the world for his lifelong service amongst leprosy patients in the name of Christ. He is co-author of the inspiring books "Fearfully and Wonderfully Made" and "Pain: the Gift Nobody Wants", subject of Dorothy Clarke Wilson's biography "Ten Fingers for God" and author of "The Forever Feast". Since 1992 Dr Brand has served as The Leprosy Mission's International President.

Evening on Galilee

Contents

Introduction

Through the gospels there is a recurring picture of Jesus eating with people, sharing the lives of his friends and followers. Sometimes he is criticised for it and often misunderstood.

When he accepts an invitation to a banquet at Matthew's home he is asked why he eats with sinners. When he is faced with more than five thousand hungry people a disciple tells him it's impossible to feed them. At dinner in Bethany there is criticism about the cost of perfume. The disciples quarrel about precedence before supper in the upper room. There is a lack of understanding among the two disciples walking to Emmaus, and hurt feelings on the beach at breakfast time as Peter is restored to his discipleship.

In each situation Jesus acts with love and insight, living out his life within the purposes of God. He faces his critics with integrity and when they are at cross purposes with him he steadfastly faces death rather than compromise; the purpose of his cross to cancel out the cross purposes of the world.

Each chapter of the book that follows concentrates on a single meal, beginning with the relevant Bible reading. Readers are then encouraged to set aside a little time to imagine the scene, to see, hear and feel something of what took place, to share in it and to meet Jesus. The chapter then continues with brief comments on particular verses and a meditation for each one.

Meditative prayer has a long and fruitful tradition in the Christian church, one that many people are rediscovering for themselves today in personal prayer and through corporate retreats. This book offers a little help along the way to any who will taste it.

Eddie Askew

Scripture quotations taken from The Holy Bible, New International Version
© 1973, 1978, 1984 International Bible Society. Used by permission.

Chapter One

SOMETHING

TO

CELEBRATE

Arab Bazaar, Old City, Jerusalem

N D ASKEW

Luke 5:27 – 32

'After this, Jesus went out and saw a tax collector by the name of Levi sitting by his tax booth. "Follow me," Jesus said to him, and Levi got up, left everything and followed him.

Then Levi held a great banquet for Jesus at his house, and a large crowd of tax collectors and others were eating with them. But the Pharisees and teachers of the law who belonged to their sect complained to his disciples, "Why do you eat and drink with tax collectors and 'sinners' ?"

Jesus answered them, "It is not the healthy who need a doctor, but the sick. I have not come to call the righteous, but sinners to repentance." '

Matthew 9:9

'As Jesus went on from there, he saw a man named Matthew sitting at the tax collector's booth. "Follow me," he told him, and Matthew got up and followed him.'

Pack horses

Luke 5:27 – 32

Take a few moments to imagine the scene.

Picture yourself among the disciples walking with Jesus. The customs house is on the edge of the busy main road, a trade route from Damascus through Capernaum to the coast and all the way down to Egypt.

It's a warm day. Outside the house is a chaos of carts and wagons carrying grain, wine, olive oil. A confusion of horses, donkeys and mules kick up the dust, their drivers shouting and quarrelling and sweating in the sun. Urchins run through the mêlée, ready for anything.

We follow Jesus as he walks through the crowd, brushing away the flies, ignoring the smells, watching where he puts his feet. He goes through the gate in the high wall, past the guards armed against robbers, and enters the courtyard. It too is crowded with reluctant tax payers.

The pillared veranda and the rooms behind shelter tables and benches, and give welcome shade to all who work there. The tables are covered with papyrus scrolls and wax tablets for note taking, invoices, bills.

Businessmen sit and argue with accountants, pleading poverty. "It's been a bad year for olive oil...I can't afford to pay." Poor men ask for mercy, not even expecting justice.

Levi sits in the main room. His secretary, a male slave, waits behind him. Jesus stands quietly in front of the table, but Levi continues to write, head down. He's a bureaucrat enjoying the taste of power in the ten second wait. Then he looks up at Jesus and as their eyes meet there is some strange compelling transaction between them. "Come," says Jesus and as Levi responds to the invitation, pushes back his chair and stands, he becomes Matthew, "Gift of the Lord".

City Walls, Jerusalem

"Follow me," Jesus said to him, and Levi got up, left everything and followed him. Luke 5:27 – 28

Matthew was a tough, shrewd and cynical tax collector, a man willing to accept deep unpopularity in his pursuit of wealth. I wonder why he gave it all up to follow Jesus. It wasn't just a weekend adventure, but a deep commitment involving his whole life.

Some suggest it was simply the attraction of Jesus' charismatic personality, some magnetism that left Matthew powerless. But Jesus never forced himself on anyone. Many people met Jesus and turned away, apparently unaffected by him. Matthew too could have said no.

Perhaps it was the fact that Jesus, this new teacher and miracle worker who was beginning to attract crowds to hear him, was willing to take him as a friend, accept him as he was. Jesus made no accusations, no recriminations. Matthew wasn't used to that. He was accustomed to being disliked and had learned to shrug it off, superficially at least, and pretend it didn't matter.

Jesus gave him a simple invitation, and offered it with love. "Follow me. Come as you are." Centuries before, Moses reminded his people of the way God had freed them from slavery in Egypt. He told them that it wasn't because they were more in number that the Lord chose them but because he loved them (Deuteronomy 7:7). Jesus was saying a similar thing to Matthew.

We can all build that into our understanding. It's not because we're better, more intelligent, harder working or even more enthusiastic that the Lord chooses us, but because he loves us. It's a plain unconditional fact. We sometimes find that hard to accept. We'd rather work for his love so that we could think we'd earned it, but that's not the way it is and we simply, or not so simply, have to accept it.

Matthew deserved nothing. His life-style had made him unacceptable to most people but that wasn't the point. Jesus offered him and offers us unconditional love. Paul Tillich once wrote: *"We need the courage to accept that we are accepted in spite of being unacceptable."*

God welcomes us, not because of anything we've done or are, but because he loves us. That's the truth and we can take it or leave it. And even if we choose to leave it he still loves us.

Sometimes Lord
I'm tempted to think
that I can earn my ticket.
Perhaps even suggest
with modesty of course
that I'm a little better
than the other man,
or woman, come to that -
although I wouldn't say it publicly -
and deserve a little more from you.
Then I come back to earth
and realise that nothing in my life's
quite as it should be.
Too many dusty corners,
cobwebs covering the cracks.
A lifetime's rubbish
cluttering the floor
of all my good intentions,
waiting for the house clearance
that never seems to come.
The things I treasure most,
and put back on the shelf
each time I tidy up,
worth nothing.

But then I hear your voice.
Gentle.
Sometimes I wish you'd shout.
Then I could fight,
try to defend myself,
but the gentleness defeats me.
"Come as you are."
No frills, no entrance fee.
Don't even need to bring
a bottle to the party.

I am accepted
not for anything I've done
but simply for myself.
It hurts my pride a bit at first,
but that's a little price to pay.

But the Pharisees and the teachers of the law who belonged to their sect complained to his disciples, "Why do you eat and drink with tax collectors and 'sinners'?" Luke 5:30

Jesus seemed to enjoy parties. When Matthew threw his, Jesus was right in the middle of it as chief guest. Matthew had something to celebrate. Meeting Jesus had changed his life, transformed his values. The only people who would eat with Matthew were other tax collectors and people from the twilight world of questionable enterprise and routine dishonesty. An ancient writer spoke of *"robbers, murderers and tax collectors"* all in the same sentence and I imagine some of the other disciples had reservations too. That didn't deter Jesus.

The 'righteous' people, the Pharisees and teachers of the law, stayed outside in a flurry of ruffled feathers. They kept their distance. They even excluded people like Matthew from the synagogue. They asked how Jesus, this centre of integrity and goodness who claimed a special relationship with God, could surround himself with people whose lives were a constant compromise with evil? They believed God only operated within the lives of those who kept every nuance of the law handed down by Moses.

They were sincere people. That was the tragedy. In trying so hard to keep the law in all its detail they'd boxed themselves in. Their rigid life-style, their harsh condemnation of others, allowed no room for grace. Grace needs to breathe the oxygen of freedom and love. It withers in an atmosphere poisoned by criticism. Their self-righteousness made it impossible for them even to recognise who Jesus was. And so grace passed them by and came to Matthew's house as Jesus reclined among the sinners and despised.

The sad thing was that those who placed themselves at the centre of religious life and society, and by their judgement pushed others to the edge, were really at the edge themselves. In Jesus the centre had shifted and those with him were at the centre. The only people the critics excluded were themselves.

It was the sinners who sat with Jesus, who enjoyed his company and felt his love. Those who kept themselves apart for God ended by keeping themselves apart from God. The 'holy' ones never got to eat with him. Think what they missed.

Lord, did they ever realise
just what they'd missed?
That in the coldness of their rectitude,
their icy certainties,
they'd left no room for love.
Forgiveness frozen out,
frost-bitten in the winter of their criticism.
A sinner's hand stretched out
would find no warmth or welcome
at their hearth.

And did they never realise
that in their ready condemnation
they judged themselves
in judging you?
Lost God by holding him too tight
within the boundaries of their rules.

Lord, save me from my certainties.
Leave me some room to doubt
my own convictions.
And when I make harsh judgements
help me to see
that you will always stand
with those I push away.
And in the pushing
I exclude myself
and no one else.

Lord, take my hand
and pull me in.
I'd like to join the meal.

Jesus answered them, "It is not the healthy who need a doctor, but the sick." Luke 5:31

Contact with Jesus is two way. Immediately after Jesus invited Matthew to join him, Matthew invited him to his home. Jesus' initiative was balanced by Matthew's. As he calls us to share his life, he awaits an invitation to share ours.

When Jesus sat down to eat with him and his friends, the critics thought that he was condoning Matthew's behaviour. It's easy to see their misunderstanding. Perhaps they'd seen it all before. A promising and idealistic young man from the provinces finds some popularity, sees the chance of wealth and influence, and begins to compromise spoilt by early success.

Jesus was neither ignoring nor accepting the way Matthew had lived, but was underlining that Matthew's only way out to something better was with Jesus. He didn't say, "Matthew, you reform, you change your life and then I'll think about taking you on." He offered his help to Matthew, then and there, held out an invitation to him to examine and change his life.

If Matthew was to be kept on the edge of acceptance until he'd changed, there'd have been no change. Change depended on his growing nearer to Jesus. And Jesus risks his own name and reputation to rescue him.

He made no excuses for Matthew's past life. He didn't say, "Everybody's doing it, it doesn't matter." In answering the critics he said quite clearly that there were things in Matthew's life that were wrong, that he was sick, and needed the healing that only Jesus could give. A healing that would penetrate every corner of his life and bring a wholeness and a balance that would transform him. And if Jesus saw a future for a man like Matthew then there's hope for me.

God doesn't keep us at arm's length until we're good enough to meet him. He scoops us in just as we are.

I stand before you, Lord,
stained hands,
mud on my feet,
all my excuses
soiled and threadbare as my clothes.
And wonder
that in the chaos of my life,
all the false starts,
wrong paths,
deliberate detours,
the door's still open
and the feast awaits.

And as I move towards the door
with apprehensive joy
I'm not quite sure
whose door it is.
Yours or mine.

I ask you,
are you letting me into your life
or are you entering mine?

I guess it's all the same.
You are the door to life
and as I enter for the feast,
once more I'm not quite sure
just who's the guest.
You or me?
I thought to honour you
but somehow,
yet again,
you turn the tables,
upset convention
and welcome me.

And in your welcome
I'm not sure what makes me marvel most
your courage
or your sense of humour.
Lord, you'll need them both with me.

**"I have not come to call the righteous, but sinners to repentance."
Luke 5:32**

The thing that hits me most in this story is not Matthew's faith in
Jesus, but Jesus' faith in him. What did Jesus see in Matthew that
made him believe it was worthwhile calling him? He wasn't the
sort of man I'd employ if I were starting a new project. I'd have too
many reservations about his background.

Years ago, when I became chief executive of The Leprosy Mission,
in a moment of curiosity I took the risk of asking for my personal
file from the archives. I thought it might be interesting to see how
people had rated me in earlier days.

In the file was a record of the first interview I'd had with an
experienced and perceptive doctor when I'd offered for service
with the Mission. He'd seen me, so the record said, as "very young
and immature but with possibilities." Thank God for that last word.
Rather than write me off and look for someone better, older and
more mature, he'd taken a risk and recommended that I be taken
on. He could see possibilities.

Jesus didn't write Matthew off. He saw possibilities in him. Jesus
has faith in ordinary human beings. He comes to ordinary, fallible
people whose motives are mixed, whose lives are inconsistent, and
invites them to share his work and kingdom. No one is outside the
orbit of his love, not even those who reject him.

And with him we become greater than ourselves. It's not a question
of manipulation. Jesus is no Svengali who pulls our strings and
works us like marionettes. Every step we take with him is
voluntary. We can always choose to say yes or no, but saying yes to
him is the way we grow into maturity.

The next time you're tempted to agonise over your unworthiness
and the weakness of your faith in him, rejoice in the strength of his
faith in you.

If Matthew came for interview with me
he wouldn't stand a chance.
Wouldn't even make the short list, Lord.

A casual appraisal
of his background and experience
and I'd write him off
without a second thought.
Hardly worth the postage stamp
to send a photocopied letter of regret.

Easy from where I sit
or stand – I need the exercise -
to see the negatives
and define the reasons for rejection.
Then turn my back.

You shame me, Lord.
It seems I stand more naturally
with Pharisees
than with you.
My inclination is to stand aloof,
persuade myself
that one day
you'll come round
to see my point of view.
But then your slightest breath
blows all my righteousness to shreds.
I stand alone and vulnerable,
no virtue to commend me.
But as the first faint whisper of despair
wraps round me
I see a space near Matthew
and realise
it's kept for me.

Let's celebrate.

Tax collectors also came to be baptised.   Luke 3:12

We sometimes make the mistake of reading stories from the gospels in isolation from each other. We wonder at the spontaneity with which Matthew left everything to follow Jesus, because read in isolation that's the way it seems.

But earlier on, when John the Baptist emerged so dramatically from the desert to prepare the crowds for Jesus' coming, tax collectors were among those who came to be baptised. He stirred their consciences and when they asked what they should do, he gave them a back to basics call to honesty and justice.

Surely the word must have spread. Every profession has its grapevine, that unofficial but very effective channel of communication that spreads news quicker than fire. Jesus had been teaching in and around Capernaum on the shores of Galilee for some time so maybe Matthew had already heard about him and wondered, already felt the seeds of doubt about his life growing in his mind, was already asking questions of himself.

Later there's the story of another tax collector, Zacchaeus. He was no worse and no better than the others but he dropped his dignity and climbed a tree to see Jesus. Zacchaeus in Jericho certainly wasn't in the same tax district as Matthew but again I wonder if he too had heard, and if his curiosity to see the man who could cause such havoc among his colleagues wasn't the result of questions straining to the surface of his consciousness. Or putting it another way, that God's Spirit was already at work in his life, planting and nurturing the unease in his mind.

The presence of God can be very uncomfortable but very constructive. And immediate. At the end of the Zacchaeus story we read that, "Today salvation has come to this house." Luke 19:9. Not tomorrow but today. Salvation wasn't a future possibility but a present reality. Something that can be lived now.

Lord, sometimes I look around
and feel that nothing's happening for good.
That we've changed gears by accident
and with a screech of pain
reversed creation.
Taken all you've made
and turned it back to chaos.

But underneath the turmoil
of our frantic world
your spirit works unseen.
A pimpernel of grace and love
unrecognised
appearing where we least expect
to offer transformation.
Beneath the seeming strange coincidence
and accidental purpose
- not strange to you
and hardly accidental -
the ferment of your recreative spirit
transforms people and events
according to some loving chemistry
I can't yet comprehend.

And as I walk today
and do the tasks in front of me
keep me within your plan.
Help me to see your hand at work.
And when I can't
give me the grace
to accept uncertainty
and live it with assurance
knowing
that in chaos or creation
your hand is in control.

Chapter Two

PICNIC

ON THE

GRASS

Spring Flowers, Mount Carmel

A.D.ASKEW

Mark 6:30 – 44

'The apostles gathered around Jesus and reported to him all they had done and taught. Then, because so many people were coming and going that they did not even have a chance to eat, he said to them, "Come with me by yourselves to a quiet place and get some rest."

So they went away by themselves in a boat to a solitary place. But many who saw them leaving recognised them and ran on foot from all the towns and got there ahead of them. When Jesus landed and saw a large crowd, he had compassion on them, because they were like sheep without a shepherd. So he began teaching them many things.

By this time it was late in the day, so his disciples came to him. "This is a remote place," they said, "and it's already very late. Send the people away so that they can go to the surrounding countryside and villages and buy themselves something to eat."

But he answered, "You give them something to eat."

They said to him, "That would take eight months of a man's wages! Are we to go and spend that much on bread and give it to them to eat?"

"How many loaves do you have?" he asked. "Go and see."

When they found out they said, "Five – and two fish."

Then Jesus directed them to have all the people sit down in groups on the green grass. So they sat down in groups of hundreds and fifties. Taking the five loaves and the two fish and looking up to heaven, he gave thanks and broke the loaves. Then he gave them to his disciples to set before the people. He also divided the two fish among them all. They all ate and were satisfied, and the disciples picked up twelve basketfuls of broken pieces of bread and fish. The number of the men who had eaten was five thousand.'

John 6:8 – 9

'Another of his disciples, Andrew, Simon Peter's brother, spoke up, "Here is a boy with five small barley loaves and two small fish, but how far will they go among so many?" '

By Galilee

Mark 6:30 – 44 and John 6:8 – 9

Quietly think over the scene. Imagine yourself there on the edge of the crowd. What do you see?

Think of the colours: the dark blue water of the lake, and the black and white pebbles on the shingle shore. Up the gently sloping hillside the grass is green, dotted with yellow flowers and the brilliant scarlet patches of anemones, because it's the time of the spring rains. Higher up, the green dulls and merges into the brown haze. Above it all, the shoulder of Mount Hermon stands high and remote, clothed in snow. The blue sky pales to a dusty gold and on the horizon there are a few scattered clouds.

There's constant movement in the crowd as people move here and there. The colours of their clothing are muted: worn white, fawn, greys and browns, the natural colours of sheep's wool and vegetable dyes. Here and there a spot of brighter colour, red or purple, marks the robe of a wealthier man, but there are not many in the crowd.

What do you feel? Do you feel the jostling crowd, the man next to you pushing for a better place? Can you feel the sun on your face, the cool breeze from the lake? Your legs are tired after the long, hurried walk. The ground's hard as you sit down.

There's the smell of hot, sweaty people close together, crushed grass, drying fish from the beach.

There's noise too. Voices from the crowd make a constant hum. People talking to each other, asking questions, protesting, arguing. Slowly the voices still. There's a pause, and you hear the voice of Jesus, firm and warm.

Dome of the Rock, Jerusalem

**"Come with me by yourselves to a quiet place and get some rest."
Mark 6:31**

They were tired. Jesus had sent the disciples out on a preaching tour. They'd returned excited by their experiences and told him all they'd done. People had heard about the healings and were coming for more, making greater demands on their time and patience, so much so that they couldn't grab a bite to eat.

The disciples were getting ragged around the edges, their tempers fraying, wondering how much longer they could cope. It seemed all right for Jesus. To them he appeared to have an almost inexhaustible supply of energy when it came to helping others, but however much they tried to live up to his example, somehow they couldn't.

They were strained to the limit. Seeing it, Jesus didn't demand more of them. He looked at them with understanding and love, accepted their vulnerability, and told them they needed a day off. A time to relax.

That seems to fit many Christians today. We're human, as the disciples were. God created us human, and if that's the way he made us then he knows we can only do so much before we get tired. Getting tired is part of human life and nothing to be ashamed of.

It's a lesson many of us find hard to learn. We get busier, burdening ourselves with more and more work and, under the dutiful face of acceptance, resentment builds. Even when we find the courage to say no to new demands we feel guilty. There's no need. Jesus understands. He's no slave driver, but a shepherd who cares for his sheep.

It's not his demands that run us into the ground, it's often the unthinking demands of others, and sometimes the unreasonable demands we place on ourselves because we refuse to accept our own humanity. "I can do all things in Christ" is only true when we are doing those things he actually wants us to do, and not the things our pride tells us we can do.

Lord, I'm tired. Exhausted.
Sometimes I wonder how I find the strength.
So much to do, so little time and energy.
And always one thing more,
nagging at the back of my mind like toothache.
Unwelcome yet hard to ignore.

I buzz around, a frantic fly
battering the window pane
until I fall exhausted to the sill.
All noise and movement but so little done.
And in the effort to respond
to all the calls that others make
I find I'm losing touch with you.
The crowds get in between.
The more I do for you
the further off you seem.
A paradox until I hear your voice,
not asking more of me
but telling me to find a breathing space,
a place to rest.

And in the quiet you are there.
No accusations,
and no suggestions that I could do more.
And as we sit together
I begin to realise that many of the demands I face
are self-imposed. They're mine.
Born out of ego,
and the guilt I feel when I can't cope
comes from my pride and not from you.

Forgive me, Lord and help me to forgive myself
because I ask more of myself than you do.
And when I'm faced with something
I just can't find the energy to do
give me the honesty to face the fact
that maybe you're not asking it of me.
You made the world,
it wasn't me
and, valued as I am,
it's you who keeps it going.

"...it's already very late. Send the people away..." Mark 6:35 – 36

"Oh no! Not more people." It had all gone wrong. The tired disciples had sailed away with Jesus, hoping for a rest. When they landed another crowd faced them, demanding their attention. I imagine the disappointment as they realised there'd be no quiet time, the resentment as they tried to raise the energy to respond.

Why had so many people come, following them round the lakeside? Some, surely, out of curiosity, to see and hear this new teacher and his followers. People looking for sensation. Others came with illness, hoping for healing. Some were devout, seeking a deeper experience of the God about whom Jesus spoke so convincingly. Some simply followed the rest.

As the afternoon wore on the disciples came to Jesus, "Send the people away," they said, "it's getting late. They'll need to go and find food." I think their motives were mixed. Behind their concern for others they were saying, "Lord, we can't cope. We're hungry too. We have needs as well."

Jesus must have taken their breath away when he challenged them to feed the crowd. They were all for getting rid of the problem by sending the people away, but Jesus asks them to find a more positive solution. It encourages me to realise that Jesus is as concerned about the crowd's need for food as he is about teaching them. After a quick feasibility study and a protest about the cost from Philip, they looked around. Interest centred on a boy and his lunch. It wasn't very much. Barley loaves were the bread of the poor. Only the well-off could afford wheat. The pickled fish was local and a big industry.

The disciples reacted in a very human way. They saw the size of the problem and it intimidated them. Philip decided there was nothing to be done and they ask Jesus to send the people home. Andrew saw things differently. He acknowledged the difficulties but started with what there was. Five loaves and two fish weren't very much but it was something to begin with. He may not have thought it through to the end but he took a much more positive line than Philip. That's the way many great enterprises have begun, with one person's willingness to have a go with what he's got. It's also the way we have to learn to cope with our own smaller problems.

Lord, trust me to see the problem.
I'm very good at that.
My talents lie much more
in demolition than construction.
I have a great ability
born of long practice
to analyse a situation,
dissect it bit by bit
and show how difficult it really is,
until I can excuse myself
convincingly
from doing anything at all.
Action impaled
on all the snags I find,
a dead insect on a pin.

Yet Lord you ask me to begin.
Reach out for what there is
and make a start.
And when I do
reluctantly,
objections only temporarily withdrawn,
you take the lead
and walking by my side
remind me, patiently,
that if I offer everything to you,
including my reluctance,
you'll take me over,
see me through.

I must admit
I still have reservations.
I don't give up as easily as that.
But maybe just this once
I'll take a breath,
commit myself
and leave the rest to you.

"Here is a boy with five small barley loaves and two small fish..."
John 6:9

No one seems to give much time to the boy. John's gospel is the only one that mentions him at all. The other three gospel writers concentrate on the food. The boy remains in shadow, with no name or personality, but to think only of the gift and not the giver leaves part of the story untold.

Children grow up quickly in peasant societies. They're given responsibilities early in life. In many Asian countries today children of five or six years old care for younger brothers or sisters while parents work in the fields. When they are eight or nine they're sent out all day to herd the goats and cattle. We don't know how old this boy was or what he was doing out on the hillside, but the fact that he had food with him suggests that he expected to be out all day. Peasants can't afford mid morning snacks.

I picture him, brown eyes bright and responsive as he hears Jesus tell the disciples to feed the crowd. The words seem to be aimed at him. He has food, not much, but something inside him responds to what he's heard. He takes it personally. We shall never know if he was the only one in the crowd who had food with him, but the important thing is that he was willing to share.

The boy stands in the crowd, surrounded by adults who pay little attention to him as they get on with the business of giving out the food, but I hope that Jesus put his arm round the boy's shoulders and thanked him. It was his readiness to offer what he had to Jesus that made the whole thing possible. His bread, his fish. That's something to think about.

I wonder what happened to him afterwards? First, as he went home at sunset and shared his story with the family. And later as he grew up and the day's events were filed in his memory, what effect did this one moment with Jesus have on him? Was it just a day's adventure, or did it change his life?

We don't know. Neither do we know the effects our words and actions have on other people. Not that that should make us scrutinise obsessively every little thing we say or do, or we should lose all spontaneity, but it does mean that we should recognise that our gifts, however small or insignificant they seem, can be offered to God. And he can use and multiply them in ways we've never dreamed of.

Lord, not much to build on
a picnic lunch
for one young boy
who you might think
would have been better off at school
than following a crowd
around the countryside.

So easy to ignore a boy,
his head below your eyes.
Not old enough
to have opinions of his own,
and much too insignificant
to affect the outcome.
Easy to talk over him
as they discuss the situation
with all the gravity
that comes with age.
Although if wisdom came with beards
we'd honour goats.
Sometimes I think we do
but that's another story.

Yet he's the one, the boy,
whose gift you used
beyond all reasonable expectations.
While they were
working out the odds
and figuring the angles
he was opening his hands to give.
It wasn't much
and yet it was enough
to start the feast.

Lord, take the little I can give.
At times I hesitate
to offer it at all
my talent seems so small.
But if my loaves and fish can be of use
I offer them with joy.
Please take them,
and in your creative love
transform both them and me.

"... but how far will they go among so many?" John 6.9

We can't see Andrew's face or hear the tone of his voice as we read his words, but I imagine a raised eyebrow, a quizzical smile, as he asks the question. Five small barley loaves and two pickled fish are not much for five to eat, let alone five thousand.

I wonder what was in Andrew's mind? Did he really think Jesus could create something positive out of the situation? Maybe he did, although the tone of the question and the *but* suggest some doubt. The need was so great it didn't seem remotely possible that this small basket of food, carried in a fold of the boy's robe, could be used to feed that crowd.

I imagine what might have happened if Andrew had gone first to talk it over with his brother Peter. Or worse, with Thomas. I hear them sucking in their breath like pessimistic plumbers, shaking their heads and saying, "No, brother, it'll never work. Don't even think about it." Instead, Andrew simply took his doubts straight to Jesus, and took the boy too.

Andrew made a habit of bringing people to Jesus. First he'd brought that same brother, Peter. Now it's this boy with the loaves and fishes. Later it would be a group of Greeks, foreigners, who wanted to meet Jesus. He seemed to see himself as a channel, pointing people in the right direction, brother, strangers, boy.

There are times when our vision is as small as the loaves. It's easy to be put off by difficulties. We see a situation that seems impossible to resolve, a need too big to meet, and all too quickly we judge it hopeless and say it can't be done. In a television comedy the boss is berating a colleague who never seems to do anything. "You never show any initiative," he shouts. "You never ask me to," comes the inadequate answer. Andrew didn't wait to be asked.

His question encourages us to have a go, however unequal we seem to the task. Encourages us to offer our small talents and experience to Jesus, to see what he can make of them. Sometimes that's all that's needed, and it works. Sometimes it doesn't and we'll wonder why. But even then we'll have the satisfaction of having tried.

Lord, it must have seemed
a pointless thing to do.
One boy, two fish, five loaves.
The arithmetic all wrong.
Impossible.
No chance of any good result.
Better to dismiss the boy
and turn away.
Try something else that promised better.

I know the feeling, Lord,
doubt taking hold and trampling down
the struggling shoots of faith.
If I'd been Andrew
the story would've had
a very different ending.
Nobody fed,
no miracle,
and nothing to record.
Forgive me, Lord
for all the times I come to you,
my mind made up.
My negatives piled high,
allowing little room for you to act.

And then forgive the times
I never come at all.
Times when I've viewed the problem
sensibly
and then decided
there's nothing anyone can do,
not even you.
Too proud to ask,
too scared to admit my need.
Help me today
to make a move,
to open up my daily life
and give a little space
to you.

...he gave thanks and broke the loaves. Then he gave them to his disciples to set before the people. Mark 6:41

It's easy to live through a miracle without recognising it.

When Jesus took the bread in his hands and gave thanks he was probably using the grace his people traditionally used, and which Jewish people still use today. "Blessed art thou, O God, King of the Universe, who bringest forth bread from the earth."

Jesus acknowledged God's hand at work in nature, sustaining and repeating the miracle of fertility, growth and harvest which we all take so much for granted. Then he broke the bread. I try to imagine people's reactions to what happened next. I feel the wonder of the disciples as they see bread sufficient for all. It was something beyond their understanding even though they were taking part in it, but it was too down to earth, too concrete to be shrugged away. This was no trick, this was real, tangible.

I feel the astonishment too among those sitting near enough to see what was happening, but I wonder how many in that great crowd actually realised what was taking place. Five thousand people being fed. Actually it doesn't say that. In male chauvinist fashion it says five thousand men, but in Matthew's version of the story we're told there were women and children there too. And remember it wasn't a man who offered the loaves and fish but a boy.

So it was a great crowd, and the people would have taken up a lot of space as they sat around in groups of fifties and hundreds. Most of them would perhaps wonder where the food was coming from, but would have no means of knowing. The miracle passed them by. There may have been something special in the air that day, but most of the people had their eyes fixed firmly on the ground – or on the bread.

Most of us only recognise miracles when they conform to our expectations. We only acknowledge them when God intervenes in our lives and works in the way we ask him to, but really if God does what we expect it's hardly a miracle at all.

It seems to me that the real miracle is not when God intervenes in our world to do the things we ask him to do, but when we begin to do the things he asks us to do. That's just what the boy did.

Lord, help me lift my eyes
above the ordinary.
An ocean of routine
laps at my feet,
and as the tide of everyday affairs
comes in
swamping my perception
there's danger I could drown,
imagination waterlogged
and lifeless.

The rhythm of my life
continues
so much the same
the wonder of it passes by
unrecognised, unnamed.
The daily miracles discounted
simply by their regularity.
Perhaps, Lord,
if just once
you'd stop the sun from rising
and leave me in the dark
I'd recognise its daily presence
for the miracle it is.
And if, as many do,
I went without a meal
from time to time
I'd value more
the wonder of the harvest.

Forgive me, Lord
for limiting your miracles,
confining them to those occasions
when you seem to intervene
specifically at my request.

And Lord,
as you wait patiently
for me to recognise your hand at work
in every minute of my day
prod me a little,
shake me from my complacency,
and help me start to live
the miracle of obedience.

Chapter Three

DINNER

IN

BETHANY

The Old City, Jerusalem

A. D. ASKEW

Luke 10:38 – 42

'As Jesus and his disciples were on their way, he came to a village where a woman named Martha opened her home to him. She had a sister called Mary, who sat at the Lord's feet listening to what he said. But Martha was distracted by all the preparations that had to be made. She came to him and asked, "Lord, don't you care that my sister has left me to do the work by myself? Tell her to help me!"

"Martha, Martha," the Lord answered, "you are worried and upset about many things, but only one thing is needed. Mary has chosen what is better, and it will not be taken away from her." '

John 12:1 – 3

'Six days before the Passover, Jesus arrived at Bethany, where Lazarus lived, whom Jesus had raised from the dead. Here a dinner was given in Jesus' honour. Martha served, while Lazarus was among those reclining at the table with him. Then Mary took about a pint of pure nard, an expensive perfume; she poured it on Jesus' feet and wiped his feet with her hair. And the house was filled with the fragrance of the perfume.'

A Gateway in Bethany

Luke 10:38 – 42 and John 12:1 – 3

Two separate stories unfold the characters of Martha and Mary and while they are different stories it may be helpful to hold them both in mind.

Picture a small room in a poor house. One meaning of Bethany is "place of the poor". Village houses were built close together, each with a few rooms round a courtyard. You stoop to enter the low doorway into the courtyard, and the leather hinges creak.

Inside, the room's clean and tidy. It's important to be clean when you're poor. Your dignity depends on it, rather than on your few possessions. And with few possessions tidiness is easier. There's not much furniture. A couple of small wooden chests against the wall and a simple low table. Some clothes lie neatly folded on the chests. Other clothes hang from pegs on the wall. An earthenware water pot stands in the corner.

The sleeping mats are unrolled for you to sit on and there are a few cushion rolls for your back.

It's a familiar place for Jesus. He's stayed here many times before. It's just a few miles from Jerusalem: far enough away for him to find an evening's peace and a bed for the night, near enough to walk back there in the morning.

It's a quiet room but the quiet is relative. Goats in the courtyard shuffle and bleat as you enter, and the chickens are disturbed. A clatter of cooking comes from the back. Martha fans the flame in the cooking stove, there's a whiff of smoke and the sizzle of fresh cut vegetables shovelled into hot oil. A knife drops onto the flagstones.

It's evening and as the sun quickly fades Mary comes in with a taper to light a few oil lamps in niches in the wall. Her shadow looms large as she bends over the lamps.

The job done she hesitates, looks towards the door to the kitchen and blows out the taper. She finds space to sit down opposite Jesus, tucking her feet under her long skirt. She has eyes only for him. She looks and listens as he talks to Lazarus.

Then Martha bustles in, hot and bothered, a frown on her face.

Masada, Judaean Wilderness

Here a dinner was given in Jesus' honour. Martha served...
John 12:2

According to some, your friends are God's apology for your relatives. Mary, Martha and Lazarus were friends of Jesus. Their home was a place where he came for a meal and a bed for the night, a place where he could relax. Sometimes we read the gospels superficially, making little effort to understand the pressures Jesus was under. The nervous energy he used in teaching, in meeting doubt and criticism. All the pressures public life brings. He needed times of quiet with friends.

Hospitality was important, and hospitality meant food for the guests, even in a poor home. Martha was a good hostess, always busy, showing her love in practical ways. Mary had a different personality, wanting to be near Jesus, even if it meant neglecting the usual customs.

During my life in India I learnt that you could sit in a village home for an hour or more talking with your host while out back his wife got the food ready. Even if it was only a glass of tea and tasted of smoke, or rice and vegetables, it was prepared with care and took time. And even when it was served the hostess wouldn't sit down and eat with you. It was far more important to stand and serve you, to fill your plate or glass and make sure you were comfortable.

It also meant the evening could end without ever talking to the hostess other than saying thank-you, and without any chance of developing a bond of any sort.

Martha was doing just what was expected of her. It was Mary who was being unconventional. It explains why Martha was upset and rebuked Mary in front of Jesus. That also tells me something about the close relationship Jesus had with these friends. The fact that Martha could take her feelings to Jesus and involve him in a family argument show how unselfconscious they were with each other. Usually when we have guests to dinner any disagreements are kept hidden until later.

I don't think Jesus was saying that Martha shouldn't feed them – I reckon we'd have had a much more jaundiced account of the evening if the disciples had gone to bed hungry – but he was saying that friendship was more important and suggesting gently that giving so much time to the food left no time to give to him.

It's one thing showing your love by doing things for people, but there are times when we need simply to sit with them and hear what they are trying to tell us.

An easy trap, Lord
to get so busy doing things for you
there's no time left
to enjoy your company.
Times when I rush around so fast
my halo's almost blown away,
and in the whirlwind of activity
I lose direction.

But when I pause
to gather breath and energy
for one more push
I realise with a sense of disappointment
you're not impressed.
You sit there smiling,
waiting for the moment
when my circlings cease
and we can give each other
a proper welcome.
Not a half nod on the run
but a quiet not so brief encounter.

The trouble is, Lord,
when I'm honest with myself and you,
I have the feeling that my busyness
is meant to keep our meetings
on a level that leaves me in control.
Your presence sometimes
seems too close for comfort.
You face me with the facts
of my infirmity and fearfulness,
and in our meeting I detect
both love and judgement.

That slows me down,
but on reflection I begin to understand
the judgement's swallowed up by love,
and I'm accepted
not so much for who I am
or what I've done,
but who you are
and what you've done for me.

**Then Mary took a pint of pure nard, an expensive perfume...
John 12:3**

It was the expense that shocked the critics. To waste all that money on a gesture. Neither Mary nor Jesus and his disciples were wealthy people. Surely there could have been a better use of money than that.

It wasn't necessary either. Martha had produced a good meal. We don't know what was on the menu but she must have cooked something special for the one who'd restored her brother Lazarus to life. That's worth more than bread and cheese.

When you look behind the comments, what were the critics implying? That less than the best was good enough for Jesus? That there was no need for Mary to go to such lengths to show her love?

Village India still preserves old customs. I remember a wedding feast to which we were invited. It was within a small Christian community and as we walked through the gate into the courtyard of the house we were welcomed by the bride and groom. They stood with a bowl of water, soap and towel, and washed our feet. It was a touching moment. It's also a very practical thing to do in countries where people walk barefoot or in open sandals on dusty or muddy roads. It was a common custom in Jesus' day and Mary was taking an everyday action and elaborating it, enlarging it dramatically, creating a parable in a way that Jesus would have understood.

It was an expensive thing to do, but if you want a gift to show your love then surely it must be costly. Not necessarily in its monetary value; maybe simply in the careful thought taken in choosing something appropriate, or in the time and care in making it. A labour of love as we say.

There was something important too in Mary's spontaneity. Sometimes the thought of criticism makes us hesitate, inhibits us from showing our feelings in case we're misunderstood. Mary's love for Jesus wouldn't be contained or controlled in that way. She loved him and she was going to show him. Perhaps too Mary is saying to us all, as she was saying to those around her, "If you love somebody show them now." You may miss the chance if you wait until tomorrow.

I stand before you, Lord
not knowing where to turn
for shame.
Your love, so freely given,
almost too much to bear,
my back near breaking
with the weight of love.
I sometimes wish
you'd give a little less
so that my response
could seem a little more.
I'm overwhelmed.

What can I give to you?
Even my faith at times
seems more theoretical than real.
I'd like to offer more than cliché.
I search the corners of my life
for something worthy,
some hidden gift,
some sudden virtue
to pour out on your feet
as Mary did.
But nothing's there,
an empty jar at most,
its scent a wistful memory.

My hands are empty, Lord,
but as I stand in front of you
at least I'll offer you
my yearning,
and hope that
as I offer it in love,
in love you'll take it
and add a fragrance of your own.

Mary wiped his feet with her hair.   John 12:3

There's a sense of great intimacy here. I feel like an intruder in this room. I almost use the phrase "two's company, three's a crowd." There's an urge to step back and leave Jesus and Mary together. It's a family moment, something the outside world doesn't usually see.

We're not told how Mary felt earlier when Jesus restored her brother's life, but here's an indication. In a surging wave of gratitude, all her deeply felt but hard to express emotions rise to the surface. They burst out like uncorked champagne, fizzing, bubbling, uncontrollable.

The perfume's more than enough but as its heavy fragrance fills the room, Mary goes further. She lets her hair down. This was something grown women only did in the privacy of home and never in front of outsiders. Mary is signalling, consciously or unconsciously, how close she feels to Jesus. It's an action that shows her confidence in him, and her love for him.

Above all it shows her trust, because in this moment of intimacy she makes herself vulnerable. She opens herself to criticism, ridicule, even rejection. A lesser man than Jesus might have pushed her away in embarrassment, anxious not to be compromised. Not him, he looks through the gesture to the truth beneath and recognises the devotion.

In opening herself so fully Mary strips away all her defences. That's the core of love – finding the courage and the confidence to hold nothing back. To offer one's self totally, with no thought about what others will think or say. Her world, her vision, in this one moment is filled with Jesus.

We're not told how Lazarus reacted but surely he, more than anyone else, would have understood why she did what she did.

Lord, cleaning up the party's
always an anticlimax.
The guests long gone
leaving their thank-yous
and their imprints on the cushions,
the dirty plates
and empty glasses
an unwelcome antidote
to all that's gone before.
A coat, forgotten,
hangs limp and lonely on a peg,
nobody's child.

Did Mary feel like that?
And did she wonder
if she'd gone too far,
the criticism adding hurt
to indiscretion?
And Martha,
apron wet from washing up,
still wondering about the cost?

Or was there still
an afterglow,
a feeling of content
that they had had
an evening like no other?
The smell of perfume
lingering,
reminding them
that love had visited
and sat
and ate
and talked with them.

Lord, touch my life like theirs.
That in the morning after
I may know that you were here.
And that there's no regret.

Chapter Four

SUPPER

IN

JERUSALEM

Olive Tree, Gethsemane

A. D. Askew

John 13:1 – 14

'It was just before the Passover Feast...The evening meal was being served...Jesus got up from the meal, took off his outer clothing, and wrapped a towel round his waist. After that, he poured water into a basin and began to wash his disciples' feet, drying them with the towel that was wrapped round him.

He came to Simon Peter, who said to him, "Lord, are you going to wash my feet?"

Jesus replied, "You do not realise now what I am doing, but later you will understand."

"No," said Peter, "you shall never wash my feet."

Jesus answered, "Unless I wash you, you have no part with me."

"Then, Lord," Simon Peter replied, "not just my feet but my hands and my head as well!"

Jesus answered, "A person who has had a bath needs only to wash his feet; his whole body is clean. And you are clean, though not every one of you," for he knew who was going to betray him, and that was why he said not everyone was clean.

When he had finished washing their feet, he put on his clothes and returned to his place. "Do you understand what I have done for you?" he asked them. "You call me 'Teacher' and 'Lord', and rightly so, for that is what I am. Now that I, your Lord and Teacher, have washed your feet, you also should wash one another's feet." '

Luke 22:24 – 26

'Also a dispute arose among them as to which of them was considered to be the greatest. Jesus said to them, "The kings of the Gentiles lord it over them; and those who exercise authority over them call themselves Benefactors. But you are not to be like that. Instead, the greatest among you should be like the youngest, and the one who rules like the one who serves." '

An Upper Room in Jerusalem

John 13:1 – 14

Put yourself among the disciples coming together for supper with Jesus. It's the Passover. Moonlight paints shadows along the narrow street, the doorways shut and dark. You feel your way up the outside staircase, a hand on the rough wall. As you go inside, the door creaks and little oil lamps glow, giving soft light to the room. Shadows leap across the walls as the small flames flicker in the draught.

You wash your hands in the bowl at the door, the water cool as you shake it from your fingers. As you sit down you hear noises from the city. There are voices in the street. A door slams, and in the distance a dog barks at the moon. There's the smell of food. Fresh baked bread, roast lamb, herbs, rough country wine.

You feel a bit uncomfortable though. It's not really a party atmosphere. You hadn't wanted to come to Jerusalem, it had seemed too dangerous, but Jesus had insisted. And there'd been an argument at the door about who'd sit where, and who was most important. Jesus had intervened. He hadn't raised his voice much, but you could hear the strength in it. He'd left you all in no doubt about how he'd felt.

"I'm here as a servant," he'd said. That was strange. It made you think. So you keep your eyes down, not yet ready to look directly into his.

What does Jesus see as he looks round the room? They're all people he loves, faults and all. Peter – hot-headed. Thomas – a bit cautious. Judas...and you. What does Jesus see in you?

Then he moves. You hear water pouring. He takes a towel and a bowl and starts to wash the disciples' feet. John's, Andrew's...Now you realise that he's coming to you. He's going to wash your feet.

Think about Jesus kneeling down in front of you, taking your foot. How does it make you feel? And as your eyes meet, what do you want to say to him?

Spires and Minarets, Bethlehem

It was just before the Passover Feast.   John 13:1

Actually the other three Gospel writers affirm that it was the Passover. Passover was and still is the meal which reminded all who shared in it that God's gift to them was life and freedom.

First he'd rescued them from Egypt where they'd been slaves to Pharoah's megalomania and taken them into the open spaces of the desert. Desert life wasn't easy but it was one in which, under God and Moses, they were free to make their own choices. But the crucial freedom God offered was a freedom of the spirit, the chance to make an inner journey of exploration which would bring them closer to him.

Their physical freedom didn't last. Once settled in the promised land, and with a deepening experience of their God, they again became prey to stronger political powers – Assyria, Babylon and eventually Rome. In Jesus' day Roman power was everywhere and he came up against it even before he was born. It was Romans who ordered the census that took his pregnant mother to Bethlehem.

But the real journey is the inner one. That's the one that takes us beyond the circumstances and constraints imposed from outside and offers us the space to experience the presence and love of God.

It's sad that in Jesus' day this people of Passover, who should have understood the value of inner freedom more than anyone else, had become so defensive and ingrown. Their leaders could offer no freedom to Jesus. Because his experience and teaching took him over the boundaries of their conventional beliefs they saw him as a danger, someone who had to be controlled.

It's not easy to understand but perhaps they'd lost so much through political oppression that they felt the only thing left to them was their faith and in a sincere attempt to protect it they'd put walls round it, made it inflexible.

However we look at it the effect was the same. The people whom God had rescued now plotted to arrest Jesus. The freed became the oppressors who turned the freedom meal into a prelude to captivity and death.

And yet that's not the ultimate sadness. That lies in realising that through their actions they judged and sentenced themselves, and stepped voluntarily into a prison of self-righteousness. In the end, rejecting God's freedom hurt them more than it hurt God.

Lord, I don't know if I want
the freedom that you offer.
It scares me.
There's comfort in conformity.
It's easier to live by rules.
No need for choice,
just follow without question
what my elders say,
my own reactions cut
to someone else's pattern
and tailored to a suit
of someone else's size.
Uncomfortable, dull but respectable,
dark grey and suitable for all occasions.
And in a way it brings release
from all the tension and the stress
of thinking for myself.

Your freedom asks so much.
Asks me to make my own decisions,
chart my own course,
accept responsibility for all I do.
To make the gradual, sometimes painful, journey
from childhood to maturity.

But when I find the courage to move out,
and take a first small hesitant step
beyond the boundaries of what is safe
I find within my ordinary life
the expanding universe of yours.
Not that the known parameters
of daily life can be ignored
but that woven within them
is a new dimension,
the glory of your presence.
The interplay excites me, leaves me breathless
and even though I'm still afraid from time to time,
I wish no other way.

Your freedom makes its own demands -
the paradox of life with you -
but Lord, I'll take the risk.

The evening meal was being served.   John 13:2

I've always thought of the Last Supper as a private meal, just Jesus and his disciples. The gospels don't mention anyone else, but a holiday in Venice changed that for me.

We visited the church of San Giorgio Maggiore, built on an island across the Grand Canal. Inside is a large painting of the Last Supper by one of Venice's master painters, Tintoretto. The picture's big in concept as well as size, and the painter's vision leaps out of the frame and hits you hard in the imagination.

It's a scene of great activity. Jesus is there, offering bread to his disciples, but there are others too. As well as angels watching from the wings as it were, there are servants carrying food and wine jars, women cooking and, if my memory's correct, a couple of dogs waiting for the leftovers.

It's really a banquet scene set in 16th century Venice, at the time the artist lived and painted. In painting it that way he was trying to make the story relevant to his day and people. It's a crowded scene, not at all as I've pictured the event, but my view's been formed by the dignity of the usual church communion service.

The painting makes me think again, makes me ask whether there were others present. St. Mark tells us in his version of the story that "the disciples...prepared the Passover." Then "When evening came Jesus arrived with the twelve." So the twelve came with Jesus; and that leaves me asking who cooked the meal? The main course in a Passover meal is roast lamb. Someone had to cook it. It was a great occasion for all, except for the lamb of course.

I'm using my imagination but with Bethany only a couple of miles away, I wonder if Martha was doing the cooking again, and Mary waiting to share another evening with Jesus, listening to his words. The plain answer is we don't know, but life isn't a series of watertight compartments, their events each separate and unrelated. There's a continuity about things, events flow one into the next even though we can't always see the relevance or connection.

But however many people there were I know that Jesus looked on them all with love, even Judas.

*Perhaps it doesn't matter, Lord
how many folk there were
to share the meal.
I like to think of it as quiet,
just a favoured few.
Or, best of all,
just you and me.
A chance to sit as Mary did
and listen,
look, and -
if you'll pardon the intrusion -
touch.
I'd like to sit with you,
the room pulled round us
close and intimate,
walled in and held secure,
cocooned against the world.*

*The more the merrier they say,
but I have problems
opening my life to others.
It seems that when the door is open
I lose control.
Rich man, poor man,
beggar man, thief,
it's all the same to you.
Your arms are open to them all.
And as I move reluctantly
to give them space
my quiet moment's gone,
shattered,
the saucepan clatter of their need
filling the room.*

*But then, Lord,
when I stop and think
I realise the only reason
that you welcome me
is that you welcome all.
If I could influence events
and keep the kingdom for the few
there'd be no room for me.*

Also a dispute arose among them as to which of them was considered to be the greatest. Luke 22:24

I can't help looking at this story through the eyes of Mary, Martha's sister, and in a way through Martha's eyes too. Whether they really were there at the supper, or only there in my imagination, they were certainly nearby and would have heard about all that happened in the room that evening.

It was the end of the day and the disciples were tired and tense, not knowing what would happen tomorrow. Just the atmosphere to breed misunderstanding and disagreement. Suddenly there's a quarrel about the pecking order, about who among them was most important. It's so easy to get things out of proportion when you're tired. It could have been no more than an argument about who should have the privilege of reclining next to Jesus. It might have been a deeper struggle about who, next to Jesus, would hold the reins of power in the coming kingdom.

It's an insidious temptation which sidles up quietly without our suspecting or recognising it. Politicians talk glibly of serving the community and indeed call themselves ministers – servants – when what they really want is the power to control others.

Christians have little immunity and even church hierarchies sometimes seem to reflect more power than service. At best our motives are mixed. Do we seek opportunities to serve because love makes us do it or does our subconscious grab at the chance of exercising a little more authority?

"There's no one else to do it" sometimes needs to be read as "I don't want anyone else to do it." It's easier to ask the question than to give an answer, but whatever bit of the church we live in the question of authority soon raises its head. And perhaps we should beware especially of those who claim their authority is God-given and exercise it in a way that Jesus never did.

Present or absent from the meal, Mary and Martha give us an insight. One was content simply to sit at Jesus' feet and learn from him, the other kept her energies to serve.

And have I hurt you, Lord
as those men did?
Do I spin webs of selfishness
which put me at the centre
of my own small world?
And are there moments
when I'm more concerned
about my own position
than I am of yours?
Times when I fight to lift myself
a bit above the rest,
enmesh you
in my egotism?

There in the upper room
the tension must have been
almost too much to bear.
A chance for them to comprehend
the height and depth
and length and breadth of love.
A chance elbowed aside,
pushed down and trampled
in the rush to take advantage.
The temple of your presence
transformed into a market place
where love was at a discount,
traded for power.

Lord, let me learn from them
and from my own mistakes.
And let me learn from you
that love can never grasp for privilege
except the privilege
of standing back
and giving way.

...and (Jesus) began to wash his disciples' feet. John 13.5

You can never predict how Jesus will act. That's one of the joys and uncertainties of following him. We try to box him in with our own rules and dogmas, but again and again he takes us by surprise.

A few days earlier, Jesus had been at supper in Bethany. There, he'd reclined at the table while Mary washed is feet, perfumed them and dried them with her hair. An extravagant picture but one in which we see a disciple honouring the teacher, the lesser paying homage to the greater.

Now Jesus turns everything upside down. It's he who lifts the jug and bowl. Jesus who kneels and takes their feet in his hands. It must have shattered them, these men who'd just been quarrelling about their own importance, to see him take on the role of servant.

I find what Jesus did easy to accept as long as I can keep it general. His action in washing the disciples' feet is a lovely image of service and humility, a parable of what the kingdom of God is all about. The last first, the first last and all the other ideals of relationship. But when I start to particularise it all, when I start giving names to those whose feet Jesus was washing, then the difficulties begin.

I think of Jesus washing Matthew's feet – that old dishonest, even if reformed, tax collector and outcast. A man unwelcome in synagogue and polite society. Then Thomas' feet – the one who had his doubts and voiced them. And most of all I find it difficult to picture Jesus kneeling in front of Judas, taking his feet in his hands with the same love he offered to them all.

I wonder how Judas felt, how his toes curled in embarrassment and guilt? Was it his body language then, his tension, that told Jesus of disloyalty and betrayal?

Sometimes I take my thoughts a little further and try to imagine my own feelings as I realise that Jesus is kneeling at my feet...

Lord, in the light
of haloed holiness
I sometimes make believe
I have a right to wear,
your truth burns hot,
blisters and scars my insincerity.
I see you kneeling there,
taking the feet of folk
who sometimes trampled on your love
without a thought.
Trod holiness into the ground and left it hurt.
Half dead, with no Samaritan to help.

Your action leaves me questioning,
teaches me more than I am ready to accept.
It's not that I protest, like Peter,
and refuse to let you wash my feet.
That's not the point.
I'd let you do that willingly
and given half a chance
I'd just as willingly wash yours.
A privilege I'd jump at.
The bit that makes me hesitate,
rubs the raw edges of my pride
and leaves me sore,
is that you're telling me to do the same.

I can accept the thought of kneeling
to the ones I love
and those who love me back.
But looking round
I'm not so sure about the others.
To go to those I find
unsympathetic, incompatible,
the ones I'd never think
of bringing home to dinner
and offering them the same consideration.
Lord, that's rough,
but if you found it in your heart
to welcome Judas
I've no excuse.
I'd better make a start.

"Do you understand what I have done for you?" John 13:12

The honest answer is, "No, we don't." None of us really understands. We may claim to, but whenever I hear a simple explanation of the life and death of Jesus I come away feeling that the speaker hasn't really understood the question.

There are so many layers of meaning to be peeled away, one by one. We can take the question simply in relation to Jesus washing the disciples' feet, its meaning in terms of service and the way we act towards one another. Beyond that we're asked if we understand his life and ministry. Then from our place in time the question asks if we understand what his death means, and beyond even that whether we really appreciate the power and significance of the resurrection and the activity of the Holy Spirit in the world today.

The question takes us into the core of faith and, for me, the only answer is, "No, I don't understand, but I'm glad it happened." And I'm comforted by the assurance in the same passage that one day we will understand.

But looking at the story I'm drawn back again and again to the thought of Jesus kneeling at Judas' feet. It's a compelling picture which vibrates with an intensity I find hard to bear because it shows starkly the reality of what love must mean. Jesus loved Judas as he loved the other disciples, and nothing Judas could do would alter that. And when Jesus prayed for forgiveness from the cross for all who had harmed him I'm sure Judas was included.

On a tour of England a few years ago, Archbishop Desmond Tutu spoke to some young people. He said, "God loves you, not because you're beautiful, although you may be. God loves you, not because you're good, although you just might be. God loves you. Full stop."

No trait of personality or behaviour can put an obstacle in the way of real love. Wherever we are, whatever we do, Jesus loves us completely, wholly, and utterly selflessly. I don't understand it, but I gladly accept it.

Lord, I come to you in wonder
as I feel your love around me.
I don't know what to say.
In ordinary circumstances
I can find a word, a phrase,
a joke to take away
the tension of the moment.
Help people relax.
But not just now.
There are moments
when the only thing that fits
is silence.
A song without word,
when the music of your life
floods over me,
leaving me breathless.

Your question echoes through my mind,
circles and returns, insistent.
No, Lord, I do not understand,
your love's too deep,
so great it almost frightens me away.
And yet each time
I try to distance it
and leave myself a little space
I find I need its strength,
and warmth and comfort.

You are too deep for understanding,
my mind too small to encompass you.
There comes a point
when thoughts can't cope,
when all the theory and theology
lie threadbare,
and the only fit response
is to fall down and worship.

Chapter Five

THE MEAL

THAT

NEVER WAS

Shepherds' Fields, Bethlehem

Luke 24: 13 – 19, and 28 – 33

'Now that same day two of them were going to a village called Emmaus, about seven miles from Jerusalem. They were talking with each other about everything that had happened. As they talked and discussed these things with each other, Jesus himself came up and walked along with them; but they were kept from recognising him.

He asked them, "What are you discussing together as you walk along?"

They stood still, their faces downcast. One of them, named Cleopas, answered him, "Are you only a visitor to Jerusalem and do not know the things that have happened there in these days?"

"What things?" he asked.

"About Jesus of Nazareth," they replied. He was a prophet, powerful in word and deed before God and all the people...

As they approached the village to which they were going, Jesus acted as if he were going further. But they urged him strongly, "Stay with us, for it is nearly evening; the day is almost over." So he went in to stay with them.

When he was at table with them, he took bread, gave thanks, broke it and began to give it to them. Then their eyes were opened and they recognised him, and he disappeared from their sight. They asked each other, "Were not our hearts burning within us while he talked with us on the road and opened the Scriptures to us?"

They got up and returned at once to Jerusalem.'

A Jerusalem Alley

Luke 24: 13 – 19, and 28 – 33

You are one of the two disciples walking home to Emmaus.

You are walking west from Jerusalem, into the bright golden glow of the setting sun. The road is dusty and winds along the brown hills that hide Emmaus from your view. There are other people on the road, busy with their own thoughts as you are with yours. Long shadows undulate over the rocky ground.

There are villagers driving their donkeys back from market where they've been selling to pilgrims up for Passover. Merchants too, in caravan, making for their first night's camp on their journey to the Mediterranean coast. A small squad of Roman soldiers tramps along, sweating in their body armour, the sun glinting warmly on the metal. Their song interrupts your thoughts briefly, then they are gone, walking much faster than you are.

It's been a strange, eventful day, after the enforced quiet of Sabbath. You'd been mourning then, finding it hard to come to terms with the death of Jesus, his body hurriedly bundled into the tomb before Sabbath began. Now you are trying to get to grips with this tale the women have brought back from the garden. They'd gone early, found the tomb empty and come back with a story of angels.

Grief does unpredictable things to people. You don't know whether to believe what you've heard or not, and your thoughts go round in circles as you talk about it.

Preoccupied as you are, you hardly notice the traveller who joins you, and give him a curt answer to his first question. But he draws you out, and you find it helps to talk, to go through the details of the last few days. He seems to know much more about the Messiah than you thought, and has the Scriptures at his fingertips. There's something familiar about him, some strange affinity between you, as though you've met before, and as you near the village, and turn down the familiar alley to the courtyard gate, you ask him in.

The words just come out. You hadn't meant to give the invitation, but somehow you want him to stay. Water to wash hands and feet is quickly ladled from the pot by the door, the table's laid with bread and wine. Your guest doesn't wait for you as host to offer food, he takes the bread, says grace, and in that moment you know it's Jesus. And he disappears.

By the Jordan

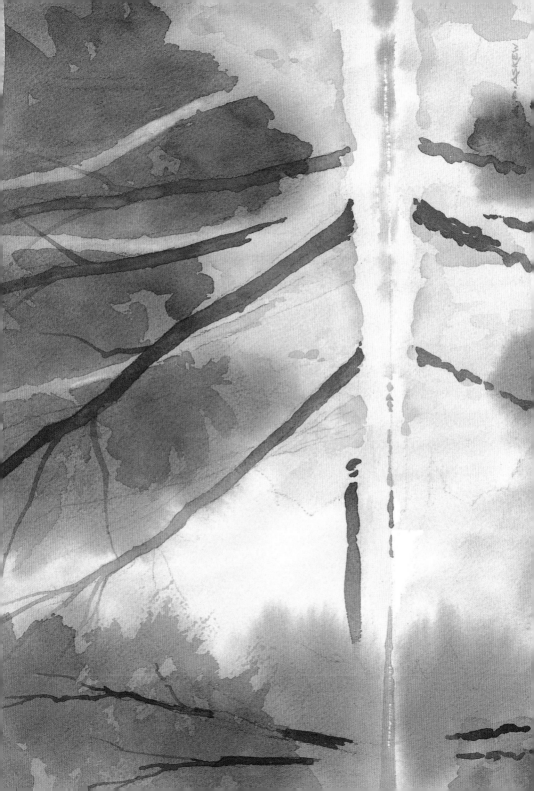

**Jesus himself came up and walked along with them; but they were
kept from recognising him. Luke 24:15 – 16**

There were three occasions when Jesus' followers failed to
recognise him after his resurrection: one with Mary in the garden,
this event, and a later one when Jesus offered breakfast to disciples
who'd been out all night fishing.

Cleopas and his companion were so preoccupied with their
problems that they didn't know him when he walked with them.
It's hard to understand, and impossible to explain convincingly.
Jesus was in their thoughts. They were talking about him as they
walked. They'd heard about the angel at the tomb saying that he
was alive, yet still they weren't prepared for his appearance.

Perhaps they were too bruised by events to take it in. Punch-drunk
by the force of the blows that had hit them, reeling from the shock
of great change, and unable to adjust to it. Their minds not simply
unwilling, but unable to take it all in. There are folk like that today.
People so battered by circumstance, so ground down by poverty or
tragedy, that good news is almost impossible to accept.

We too experience it in one way or another. Someone's said that
change is the only certainty in today's world. I believe there are
other certainties, but it's a point worth making. Few of us like
change; it makes us insecure. We prefer the known, the familiar.
And it's hard to make sense of some of the social, moral and
political changes we're living through. The pressures of coping
increase and it's difficult to see any good in many of them, but it's
important to realise that Jesus is walking with us through the
changes.

It's important too to recognise that sometimes he's in the change
itself; that the Holy Spirit may create change to stretch us, make us
face reality and grow. The cross itself was change, radical change,
and without it there'd be no future for the two walking to Emmaus,
nor for us.

Sometimes his presence helps make sense of the changes that
come; sometimes even with him it's hard to understand their
purpose, but his presence is the essential thing to hold on to.

With him, things make sense, eventually. Without him, they never
will.

Forgive me, Lord,
for all the times
I walk through life head down,
my vision limited to the immediate.
Confined within the pressures of my day
problems press in,
expand,
prevent the recognition
that we both desire.
I find it hard to look beyond the obvious,
my mind so sealed
it almost breaks imagination's fingernails
to prise it open
to the wonder of your presence.

Yet still you walk with me,
each step a revelation of your love,
a gentle leading on
to boundaries of understanding
I've not yet crossed.
Have patience, Lord.
Help me to see
your hand at work
shaping my life,
and make your nearness a delight
that turns my mourning into joy.

"He was a prophet...but we had hoped..." Luke 24:19 – 21

Cleopas and his companion were living the past. "He was a prophet," they said. All their grief and disappointment were held in that one word. Whatever their hopes and aspirations had been, they'd all gone with the death of Jesus. "We had hoped.." they said, but not any more. Their world was in ruins.

We know little about Cleopas and the unnamed companion with him, other than this story. We don't even know whether the anonymous one was a man or a woman. It's often assumed that they were two men, but it doesn't say so. It could well have been a man and his wife going home to Emmaus; that would explain the ease with which they invited Jesus to stay with them. We don't know how they came to Jesus, or how close they had been to him. The connection must have been reasonably close because at the end of the story, when they went back to Jerusalem, they knew where the leading disciples were and were able to go straight to them to tell them what had happened.

I imagine them on the road to Emmaus, preoccupied with the apparent catastrophe of the crucifixion, their minds full of regrets. If only... If only Jesus hadn't come to Jerusalem for Passover; if only he'd been more tactful with the priests and money changers in the Temple; if only he hadn't gone into the garden after supper; if only someone had realised what Judas was up to...

And now it was all done and gone. There could be no retracing of steps, but they had no thoughts about what lay ahead. Yet as Jesus began to walk with them, things started to make sense. Slowly and gently he showed them the significance of what had happened. He helped them to put the past together in a way that they could build on, and by the time they'd reached Emmaus they were ready for the future. A future that began around the table with him, their eyes open, their faith renewed.

And it was a future which led them, and leads us, not to a setting sun at the end of the day but to the dawn of a new beginning.

Lord, as I try to build my life today
a few bricks at a time
help me to build it on reality.
To face the present with the courage
only you can give.
It's tempting now and then
when life's a little rough -
I try to keep it in perspective, Lord -
to look behind,
imagine life was easier,
grass greener,
than it is today.
So tempting, Lord
to let nostalgia rule,
to play the tapes
that tell me life was better then,
and try to turn my back on now.

Lord, help me face the day.
Help me to seize the time
and shake it
'til the joy it holds
spills out
and fills my life.
Help me to sense your presence on the road,
and in those moments
when I seem alone
give me the faith that says you're there.

"...a prophet, powerful in word and deed before God and all the people." Luke 24:19

Prophets had had a powerful influence on the nation of Israel, not so much in foretelling the distant future as in telling forth the will of God. They stood with their experience and vision firmly anchored in the present, but with a sensitivity and clear-sightedness that enabled them to discern the will and purposes of God in all that was happening.

They stood with the poor and oppressed, and cried out for mercy and justice, and the uncompromising standards of behaviour they set passed judgement on both people and leaders. That made them unpopular, and no doubt they were accused of mixing religion and politics as such folk are today.

But although the prophet stood firmly in the present he looked forward to a final judgement, a day when God would bring all things to a climax and establish his kingdom. So while the prophet helped people interpret the realities of the day, he also set their minds on the future with God.

Within the limits of his understanding, Cleopas was right. Jesus was a prophet, one who discerned God's will clearly and proclaimed it fearlessly. One who freed people from their past and offered them a future.

Recently I stood on Mount Carmel, in Israel. It's a high place, as the Bible says, a sun-drenched area of jagged rock, the whole of the Jezreel Valley spread out below it. It was here that Elijah turned words into action against the priests of Baal, a bloody encounter that has to be kept in its Old Testament context to come to terms with. But it crystallises the work of the prophet, the fearless proclamation of the truth, and the need to turn word into deed. Our deeds set the seal on our words, and without deeds words accomplish little.

Jesus showed this. His teaching on love and forgiveness, on compassion for the oppressed and underprivileged, would be nothing more than an attractive and idealistic philosophy if he hadn't lived it and been willing to die for it, and for us. The word and the deed go together. Our calling is not just to preach but to act, to live out our words in what we do.

Your truth shines bright, Lord,
dazzling,
chasing away the shadows of my hesitation.
Stands stark,
confronts me in uncomfortable clarity.
And what you ask
highlights the gap
between the wish and the reality.

Easy to say
that deeds must match my words,
harder to take into my life -
consistent only in its inconsistency -
and live it out.
I'd rather leave it to the prophets,
driven ones,
who had to speak for you
whatever it would cost.

The trouble is
however hard I try
I find I cannot turn my back.
However deeply I submerge your words
within the depths,
they rise again, insistent,
telling me that word and deed are
twins who live together,
each incomplete without the other.

Lord help me find the courage
and the joy
that with glad energy
I may work out my words
in life and love.

Jesus acted as if he were going further.   Luke 24:28

Jesus acts with what Mother Julian of Norwich, writing six hundred years ago, calls "his exquisite courtesy". He's walked with them on the way to Emmaus, he's listened and talked to them with great patience, and now he leaves the next move to them. As they stand outside the gate he begins to move on.

Apparently he was willing for them not to recognise him, and wasn't prepared to put them under any sort of pressure. He'd encouraged them to see things in a different light and helped them to a better understanding, but he hadn't pushed them beyond their power to respond. He was willing to step back and give them the space they needed. He doesn't force his presence on them, but allows them the opportunity to make their own invitation.

But they asked him in. Urged him, the story says. There must have been some recognition, a picking up of signals their conscious minds had missed, which made them reluctant to let him go.

Then, as they gathered round the table, Jesus took the initiative. He took the bread, said grace, and broke it. There's an echo of that Thursday evening's supper in the upper room. There's no evidence to show that these two were present then, and no evidence that says they weren't, but in the simple act of sharing the bread they recognised him. The truth of his new life dawned on them and their new life began.

He disappeared. The story says no more. He'd done all that was needed; comforted them, shown them that he was alive. From now on they'd have to learn to live their own lives as we all do. And in their joy the meal is left unfinished. Perhaps stuffing a piece of bread into the folds of their robes and grabbing a few green olives they jumped up and began the seven mile walk back to Jerusalem. Too excited to be tired, ignoring the dangers of the dark night on the road they went back to share their news with the others.

Still standing there, Lord,
at the door,
waiting an invitation?
That you should wait for me
seems highly inappropriate.
Your gentleness is hard to take,
your courtesy too easily ignored.
If only you would push a bit,
compel me to conform,
knock louder, more insistently,
I'd listen more
open my world to you
without such hesitation.

But then I realise
your love is such
you'll never force yourself
into my life.
The choice is mine.
I'm free to open
or to close the door
and when I do -
close it I mean -
and you move on,
I know that you'll be back
patient beyond belief
to wait again
until I choose
to ask you in
and eat with me.
And then the bread and wine
take on greater significance
than I have ever known.

Chapter Six

BREAKFAST

ON THE

BEACH

Galilee Sunrise

A. D. ASKEW

John 21:1 – 17

'Afterwards Jesus appeared again to his disciples, by the Sea of Tiberias. It happened this way: Simon Peter, Thomas (called Didymus), Nathanael from Cana in Galilee, the sons of Zebedee, and two other disciples were together. "I'm going out to fish," Simon Peter told them, and they said, "We'll go with you." So they went out and got into the boat, but that night they caught nothing.

Early in the morning, Jesus stood on the shore, but the disciples did not realise that it was Jesus. He called out to them, "Friends, haven't you any fish?" "No," they answered.

He said, "Throw your net on the right side of the boat and you will find some." When they did, they were unable to haul the net in because of the large number of fish.

Then the disciple whom Jesus loved said to Peter, "It's the Lord!" As soon as Simon Peter heard him say "It's the Lord," he wrapped his outer garment around him (for he had taken it off) and jumped into the water. The other disciples followed in the boat, towing the net full of fish, for they were not far from shore, about a hundred yards. When they landed, they saw a fire of burning coals there with fish on it, and some bread. Jesus said to them, "Bring some of the fish you have just caught."

Simon Peter climbed aboard and dragged the net ashore. It was full of large fish, 153, but even with so many the net was not torn. Jesus said to them, "Come and have breakfast." None of the disciples dared ask him, "Who are you?" They knew it was the Lord. Jesus came, took the bread and gave it to them, and did the same with the fish. This was now the third time Jesus appeared to his disciples after he was raised from the dead.

When they had finished eating, Jesus said to Simon Peter, "Simon son of John, do you truly love me more than these?" "Yes, Lord," he said, "you know that I love you." Jesus said, "Feed my lambs."

Again Jesus said, "Simon son of John, do you truly love me?" He answered, "Yes, Lord, you know that I love you." Jesus said, "Take care of my sheep."

The third time he said to him, "Simon son of John, do you love me?" Peter was hurt because Jesus asked him the third time, "Do you love me?". He said, "Lord, you know all things; you know that I love you." Jesus said, "Feed my sheep." '

Fishing Boats in Galilee

John 21:1 – 17

In imagination put yourself in the boat as one of the disciples.

Listen to the water, the small waves slapping against the wooden hull of the boat. Hear the boat creak with every movement. The shuffle of feet as your companions stretch and change position.

Can you feel the boat rock as they move? There's little comfort in a small fishing boat. The thwarts you sit on are hard, unyielding. There's limited space for seven men with their nets and baskets, the sails and oars, and all the other equipment they need. After a night's fishing you are cold, sore and tired, your back aching, your knees stiff. You're hungry too.

You sit quietly. Conversation was exhausted hours ago. There's just an occasional gruff direction from Peter, in charge of the family boat. Sounds are muted in the early morning mist. You can see little, your world one of insubstantial grey.

It isn't a very positive morning. Up all night, the fishing poor, and underlying it all a lack of purpose. Life had been so full with Jesus. Now you're off balance, still reeling with all the events packed into the last few days. What will you do? The future isn't clear. Will you go back to fishing full time and take up the threads of ordinary life, or wait and see?

Then slowly, imperceptibly at first, the mist begins to thin out. The shore shows insubstantial. And then on the shore you see a vague blur, the outline of a figure. A voice calls, asks about the fishing, then tells you to throw the net once more. Suddenly you're engulfed in a great burst of activity, fish splashing water everywhere. You pull on the net, it moves, stops, moves again then stops, too heavy to lift.

A little while later you are sitting on the sand. You pull your cloak around your back, still cold from the water, but the fire slowly begins to warm you. You put your hands out to it, and rub the warmth back into them. Can you smell the smoke, the warming bread, the fish grilling?

Then Jesus offers you a piece of bread. Taste it...

Church of the Shepherds, Bethlehem

... but that night they caught nothing. John 21:3

Some things are hard to believe. This frightened group of men and women we call the disciples were bewildered. They'd gone through the horror of watching Jesus die in gut-wrenching agony, and afterwards they'd run through a whole range of emotions. There'd been shock, hurt, grief and anger at his death. It had shattered their world. They hadn't understood when he'd warned them of his coming death and they couldn't understand it now.

They'd had to deal with a sense of guilt too. They'd run away, abandoned him to face it all alone. Left him when he'd needed them most.

Then they'd had the astounding news of his resurrection. They'd seen Jesus alive again. Once more I sense a mixture of emotions. Good news is hard to believe when you're depressed, but his appearances had left them in no doubt, except for Thomas and even he'd been convinced later.

Yet still they had no clear sense of purpose, no idea of what to do next. So, back in Galilee, they went fishing. That was something they knew, felt safe about, and it gave them something to occupy the long hours of the night.

I suspect it was also a time for heart-searching. They'd left home three years ago with great anticipation. This new prophet was worth giving up regular jobs for, and there'd been plenty to do, exciting, sometimes dangerous things. Events to make the adrenaline flow. Now it was all gone. They were redundant, with all the feelings of let-down and uselessness that can bring.

It was a dark night for them, out on the water, and the enveloping mist must have emphasised their sense of isolation. Yet at their lowest point, their empty nets a metaphor for their empty lives, Jesus is there on the shore. They can't see him but he's there, sharing the dark hours, waiting to welcome, warm and feed them round the fire, ready to point them in a new direction.

Empty nets, Lord.
Moments when the strands
that keep my life together
seem tenuous,
thin threads incapable
of holding anything of note.
My fishing futile,
with nothing much to show
for all I've done.

I sit with Peter and his friends,
cold in the dark,
my mind's amalgam of
faith and uncertainty in equal parts
with hope and fear,
not knowing what's for best,
what my next move should be.
Times when I sit alone
human and very vulnerable,
boat drifting in an early morning mist
of fearfulness
net snagged on disappointment.

And yet you're there,
walking the edges of my life.
Calling me to one more effort,
your presence tempering the dark,
your sunrise scattering the mist.
And when I move
to try again
your early morning promise
offers me warmth and welcome,
and the reassurance
that my life is lived with you
and the darkness and the mist
don't count.

Early in the morning, Jesus stood on the shore... John 21:4

Luke the disciple tells us of Jesus' first contact with Peter. Jesus was on the lake shore surrounded by people, crowding him, eager to hear his words. Drawn up on the shingle at the water's edge were two boats. One belonged to Peter who was there washing his nets. Jesus got into the boat, asked Peter to row out a little from the shore and Peter's new life began.

We're not told in so many words but is seems pretty certain that Jesus is standing on the same shore again as he calls to Peter and the others at the end of their bad night's fishing. When Peter left Jerusalem for Galilee, where else would he go but home? And when it came to organising a night's fishing surely he'd take his own family boat, drawn up on the section of beach the family always used. The place where they draped their nets over the rough grey rocks to dry, where they sorted and sold their fish.

After three years with Jesus, Peter and the others were back where they began. I can almost hear the voices of neighbours gently, or not so gently, mocking. "Back home again? That was a waste of time, wasn't it? Three years away and nothing to show for it? You should've stayed here fishing like the rest of us."

Words like that must have echoed through their minds that night as they fished in the dark. Three years wasted, and all that effort gone for nothing. They were back where they began. Then through the early morning mist, before the sun rose above the high shoulders of Mount Hermon, Jesus called and asked about fish. Their answer, "Nothing", must have emphasised the waste of time. Then came the moment when they threw the net again and the water boiled with fish, the net so full they couldn't lift it in.

Did Peter think back to that first encounter with Jesus? Then too he'd put out a net when Jesus had told him to and caught so much fish that the net had torn. And that had been the beginning of his life as a disciple.

Now in the echo of that first experience Jesus was helping Peter to put behind him all the disappointment, all the pain and guilt of his denial, and take new heart. This was the beach where Jesus first called Peter and where his new life began. Now on the same beach Peter is renewed. He could start afresh, the past behind him. And that promise holds for you and me. However bleak the future looks life can begin again.

The damp breeze bites
at my back, Lord.
Strikes to the bone.
I shiver
in the morning cold of memory,
of things not done,
and others done
I'd rather not have done.
My net draws in regrets
I'd rather leave submerged.

And yet your morning presence
reassures.
Your love glows
warmer than the fire,
chases the chill.
Tells me that what's behind
can stay that way.
That memory will never come between
your face and mine.
In offering me the bread and fish
the past's wiped out,
the present precious,
the future in your kingdom.
Life can begin again,
the taste of love
more than a memory.

When they landed, they saw a fire of burning coals there with fish on it, and some bread. John 21:9

There's something very earthy and real about Jesus in the Gospels.

Whenever I look at old master paintings of the Christian story I'm struck by one thing. It's nothing to do with the composition or drawing or colour, but the fact that Jesus is almost always portrayed in spotless white robes. Whether he's depicted teaching by the lakeside, performing a miracle, or chasing traders from the temple, he's always radiantly clean.

This worries me a bit because I don't believe it could have been true. Jesus walked dusty Galilean tracks and squelched through Jerusalem mud in the rainy season. He sat on rocks to teach and in working fishing boats. There were times when he slept out on the hillside. Remember his comment about foxes having lairs and birds nests, but that he had nowhere to lay his head? (Matt.8:20)

Here on the beach he must have made the fire and gutted the fish. The hands that welcomed the tired disciples were not neatly manicured but work-worn, with dirt under the finger nails. He had the smell of fish on them, and the tang of wood smoke on his tunic.

Jesus was part of the real world, and he calls us to be the same. Involved. Sometimes I suspect I'm more inclined to stand aside and keep my hands and clothes clean, unblemished by the world. I believe Jesus would rather see the honourable stains of service, my clothes dirtied in an honest attempt to get involved.

Another thought that crosses my mind is equally challenging. It's the realisation that Jesus comes into my world not neatly starched and ironed but travel-stained, smelling of smoke and fish, or their modern equivalents, in guises I may not instantly recognise. I must take care I never let him pass by unrecognised.

I see your hands, Lord,
by the fire.
Hands of a craftsman
calloused by carpentry,
gentled by compassion.
Healing hands that touched,
turned life around.
Hands of the word made flesh
making flesh new
and spirit too.
New worlds of hope
created by your presence.

I see your hands
smoothing rough wood,
its splinters speaking
of invasive nails to come.
A time your craftsman's hands
nailed to a tree
would carve and plane forgiveness
from the agony.

I see your hands.
Hands that turned water into wine,
turned simple fish and bread
into a banquet.
And now you turn to me
offering the bread,
inviting me to take and eat
and share the meal with you.

My hands reach out in awe,
the small frustrations of the day forgotten.
And like those men around the fire
I dare not ask
"Who are you Lord?"
I know.

...the net...was full of large fish, 153, but even with so many the net was not torn. John 21:11

I wonder who counted the fish? It seems so out of place at such a time. After the cold dampness of a disappointing night's fishing the disciples land a great catch. Not land it exactly, the net's too heavy to haul aboard. As they try to deal with it and make the net secure they realise that the figure appearing out of the mist is Jesus. He's still with them, still concerned about them. Above all he really is alive. This is another confirmation of the fact, if they still needed one.

They don't know how to react. There's a suppressed excitement, a sudden tension about them. It's broken by Peter splashing ashore in his eagerness. He leaves the boat, his boat, to the others, all else forgotten as he staggers up the beach. They follow to find breakfast around the fire and Jesus serving them.

The excitement gives way to a quiet joy as they eat, their eyes following Jesus as he moves among them. Their Lord is here, not dead and gone but vital, radiant with new life. He's strong too as he challenges Peter to renew his commitment.

And at a time like this someone counts the fish. "One, two, three...hang on a minute, Lord...four, five...that's a big one...six, seven, eight..." Did it really happen that way? Probably not. It's more likely to have been afterwards when Jesus had left them, that as they began to wrap the morning up in memory someone went for another look.

Still, I find it hard to think that counting fish was a priority moments after being in the living presence of Jesus. The number of fish doesn't seem such an important issue.

It's easy to get side-tracked by things that don't matter very much. We get tempted down blind alleys when we should be concentrating on essentials. We need to use our time and energies well and on the things that will make a difference.

There have been some weird and wonderful interpretations of the number of fish. None of them seems very likely. For me it's enough to hold on to the assurance that however many fish there were the net wasn't torn. It's enough to say that the kingdom of God is strong and wide enough for all who are ready to commit themselves to living within it. There was room enough for Peter in spite of earlier denials; room for the disciples even though they'd run away in fear; and there's room in it today for you and me, and even for those I disagree with. And, however much of a strain my presence puts on it, the net stays whole.

Forgive me, Lord
for all the times
I'd rather count the fish
than face the truth.
Times when I turn away,
avoid your gaze
and hide myself
in things of little worth.
Blank out the awkward questions
that your presence brings,
ignore the challenges
and hope they'll go away,
swim back into the depths
and leave me as I am.

I much prefer the beach
and breakfast
to the storms at sea,
the times that put my words to test.

But Lord, when all is said and done
your kingdom
is the only place for me.
Throw out your net once more
and though I struggle still
wrap the firm mesh of love
around me tight,
and hold me firm.

Jesus came, took the bread and gave it to them, and did the same with the fish. John 21:13

I see these damp, weary men with looks of wonder on their faces as they gather round the fire. They sit on the hard sand, their hands out to the warmth, the cold morning air sending shivers down their spines. Or maybe it wasn't just the cold air that did it. They were face to face with Jesus, who had died but had now returned to them, life renewed.

We can only guess what was going through their minds, but I hear echoes. Echoes which reminded them of their first meeting with him on this beach, and of the joy and enthusiasm with which they'd abandoned themselves to Jesus. And as they watched him take the bread and offer it to them they must have caught an echo of the supper in the upper room back in Jerusalem. Then, as they took the fish, there were reminders of that great crowd of people on another shore not far away whom they'd helped Jesus feed. Perhaps we can take it just a little further and wonder if they heard yet another echo of the way he'd washed their feet, and now had cooked their breakfast?

There'd be personal echoes too, memories of small intimacies they'd treasured. A word of encouragement he'd given them, a hand put out when they'd stumbled on a rock.

In a little while Jesus would have something to say to Peter, words he wouldn't find particularly easy to hear or respond to, so Jesus offered breakfast first. It's a lovely touch, an authentic bit of detail, which shows so perfectly his understanding of human nature.

There are few things worse than facing a crisis on an empty stomach, particularly if you've been up all night. Jesus knows the way we're made because he was human too, and before he asks Peter to confront the issue of his failure and build something positive on it he makes sure he isn't hungry. Here was a thoughtfulness we might do well to take to heart in dealing with our families, friends and colleagues; to choose the moments of confrontation carefully and with great sensitivity.

So many echoes, Lord,
so many memories.
Times when your presence
seemed so real, so close.
Days when the hills I climbed
shouted for joy
and summits could be reached with ease.
But other echoes too
reverberate along mind's galleries.
Mornings – and nights -
when mists of doubt
drifted around my boat,
enveloped me.
And, sense of direction lost,
I've not known where to turn.
And even when I've heard your voice again
come gently through the gloom
I've found the net
too heavy still to lift.

Yet through it all
you feed me,
and offer me
a place beside the fire.
And if I feel you have
removed yourself a little way
I know it's only that you're calling me
to follow.
To make an effort,
stir myself
and move again.
Closer.

Peter was hurt because Jesus asked him the third time, "Do you love me?" He said, "Lord, you know all things; you know that I love you." Jesus said, "Feed my sheep." John 21:17

Jesus asks Peter, "Do you love me more than these?" These what? "Do you love me more than you love your friends here?" "Do you love me more than they do?" "Do you love me more than you love your past life or your fishing?" It's not really clear exactly what Jesus was asking but whichever it was there could only be one answer. Loving Jesus comes first and love changes things.

Peter must have been a ragbag of conflicting emotions. Uncertain about the future, he couldn't work out what his relationship to the risen Jesus would be; and underneath his joy at the Lord's reappearance the memory of his denial still lurked. Guilt was washing through Peter's life like water in the bottom of the boat. He'd promised earlier, boasted, that even if everyone else deserted Jesus he wouldn't. But the stark truth was that he'd failed. In the flickering light of another fire, in the courtyard of Caiaphas the high priest, Peter had turned away.

Jesus had forgiven him, the end of this story proves that. The problem was that Peter was finding it hard to forgive himself. What he'd done was something he'd have preferred to have forgotten but he couldn't. I can imagine the sick feelings surfacing as Peter lay awake in the early morning every time a cockerel crowed.

The only way forward was to recognise and face the core of the problem, which was Peter's relationship to Jesus, and the question confronted that. It hurt Peter, but growth often comes through hurt. Jesus was helping Peter search every corner of his life and renew his commitment without reserve, and then offered him a chance to build something positive from it. "Feed my sheep" is the gift of new responsibility. Christian commitment isn't to a nebulous theory or principle but to a person who calls us to a practical life of service. We show our commitment in how we live and we are shown our acceptance by what he asks us to do.